Me, Myself and My Story

By Laura A. Katz MD

Table of Contents

Introduction

My name is Dr. Laura Katz. I wrote this book for the purpose of not only sharing the details of my life thus far, but also as a salute and an empowerment boost to those out there who have gone through all the "stuff" and still come out shining. This one's for you!

Chapter 1: And now, we begin

On a cold December day, Dec 4th to be exact, a squalling blue babe was born. It was December 4th, 1969, in the middle of Detroit at Grace Hospital, which no longer exists. It is said that I came out silent and blue as blue jeans. But, after a good smack by the gynecologist, I started bawling my head off.

Thinking that my blueness meant that I was hypoxic, my father was noted to have said, after the crying and the color returning to normal, that maybe if that hadn't happened, I would have really been somebody someday. I think he was assuming that I was going to be mentally deficient someday and that they just had to hope for the best.

To add to that, after the return of normal color and the bawling, I seem to be late on attaining every last landmark. I was late getting my teeth. I was late to sit up. I was late to start to walk. I was even late in starting to talk. But, when I did, my first words were a full sentence. I literally said Hi, dad to my dad while looking over my mom's shoulder as she was carrying me upstairs. So, see, there may just have been hope for me yet.

Chapter 2: My father

I am going to forewarn you, that this will be forever referred to as my daddy fan page.

My father was an amazing man. He was a man that truly evolved. He took himself from a boy that was barely going to graduate from high school because he was allowing his environment to get him down to a man that became a teacher of every grade from first through high school, a college professor, and an author! And, along the way he became a husband and my father too. Let's be honest. That is a ton of progression.

So, according to my dad's friends, he wasn't supposed to even meet my mother in the first place. He was going on a double date with a friend, and the friend was supposed to go out with my future mom, but he wanted to trade with my dad, so my dad did. There you go, the first step in the direction of my future creation.

I think that my mother was supposedly almost engaged to someone else, in fact. However, he ended up falling in love with her and they got married, and then they had me. Welcome to the world, Laura Katz.

My dad was amazing. He was crazy smart. He had a love of humor and words. We would talk and laugh for hours all the time. I am pretty sure he also gave me the gift of superior spelling skills, which led me to win a number of spelling bees.

He had a love of all things vintage and old. He introduced me to the beatles to the point that I developed a decades-too-late crush on Paul McCartney. We copied those Beatles movies on VHS and watched them over and over.

He also had a great love of 50s and 60s music. There was always Beach Boys or Jackie Wilson or the Contours blasting at our house while we would dance around and my mother would end up excusing herself with a huff and leaving.

He also loved sports, and I did too. We would watch the Detroit Tigers religiously and the Pistons, too. I can remember being late to a violin lesson because we were watching the last game of the 1984 series on pins and needles. Wow, what a series! I literally saved every clipping from the beginning of the season to the end. I also still have my vhs tapes of the back-to-back Pistons National Championships wins in 1989 and 1990. Vinnie Johnson's final ally, oop, will be forever etched in my brain.

Sometimes, I secretly think he was hoping for a boy because he taught me all the boy kind of stuff, too. You know, cars, outdoor activities, how to fix things around the house. I was good with and into all of it.

Turned me into a handy adult. In fact, to this day, I am kind of the house handyman.

Sadly, he left this planet too early in 2008. I still miss him every day, but I like to think that he sends me little hints that he is still watching out for me. I am certain that he is the one who hides little important things when I am over-focusing on the wrong thing until I get back on track and they magically appear again. That is definitely his prankster style.

Chapter 3: The baby and toddler years

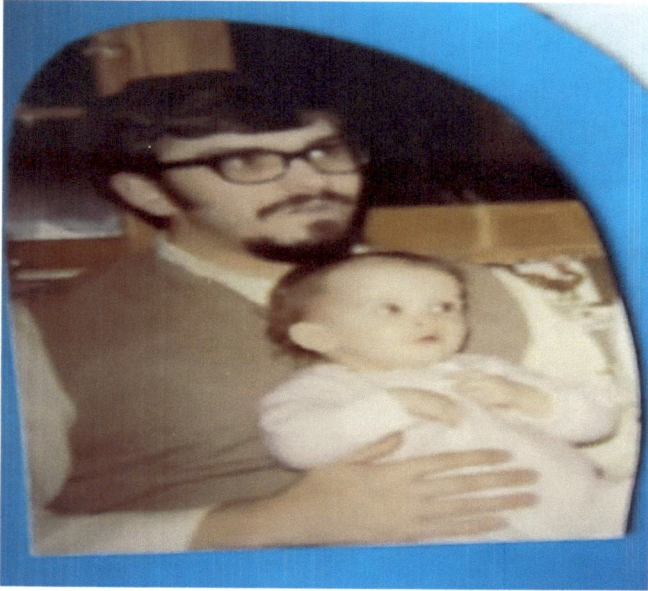

There are many adorable pictures to prove that I was indeed an awkward-looking, large, fore-headed baby, but somehow adorable despite this. I had a winning smile. I seemed to be able to charm any room. I could now walk and run like a champ. I loved to play. I have many pictures of being held by my parents with a big smile on my face, and then also an equal number when I appeared very distressed by something. Not sure what to make of that. I also have a lot of pictures of me being extremely bundled up, even in the best of weather. Not sure what they were trying to protect me from.

I know that I had a great bond with my father. Every picture that I have of him holding me when I was a baby or toddler has both of us grinning ear to ear like we had just been up to something mischievous. I think we were two plotters from the start. He was always a prankster, and I think I have definitely inherited that from him. I still hold on to that trait to this day.

I hear that my mother used to brag about me a lot. Despite all the late landmarks achievements, she "just knew" from the moment that my first words were a whole sentence that I was truly advanced. She told everyone she could about all my latest accomplishments. I hope to this day that that is just because she was so proud of me. But now, as an adult, I worry that everything just became a matter of competition between her and her relatives and friends rather than being proud of me.

I hear that I was well behaved even at the pediatrician's office. I saw this little old pediatrician named Dr. Shuck who worked in this awesome fresh 60s building near our house. I liked her. She would always pretend to be looking for Grover or some other character from Sesame Street as she was looking in my ears. It was a fantastic technique to get me to sit still so she could get good luck. I couldn't wait to see what she would find. She was one of the good ones, for sure. At times, it was hard to understand her English, but I didn't care. I couldn't wait to go see her to find out if Grover or Big Bird was in my ears that day. As far as checking my throat or anything else, I was a known gagger, so the visit would kind of go downhill from there. But, still, no crying that I know of.

Chapter 4: My tonsils

When I was two years old, I had to have my tonsils out. Back in the 70s, having recurrent episodes of strep throat was like an automatic indication for tonsillectomy and adenoidectomy. Yes, I had multiple episodes of strep throat, so of course, out they went.

Man, just like the Bill Cosby comedy record says, they build you all up, promising all the ice cream you want without telling you about the literal bomb that goes off from the time of the very first swallow after surgery. Wow, the pain is intense. I hear it is even worse if you get it done as an adult. It's hard to imagine. I have vague memories only of the throat pain and pictures of me in a lawn lounge chair with a popsicle. Apparently, I was very dehydrated from all the vomiting from the strep, and I was a poor IV stick, so they had to put the IV in my foot, and I kept begging them to take off the "sandal." Now, I get it. The sandal was the IV in my foot. Ah, it all makes sense now.

Chapter 5: Only Childhood

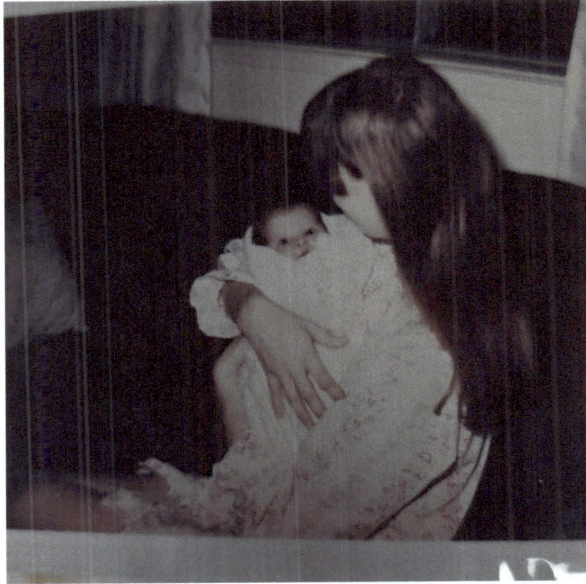

I was an only child. This is a double-edged sword in some cases. On the one hand, it means that you get all the attention and all the potential holiday presents. It means that you are the only person your parents have to spend money on so chances are that you could get luckier than most with gifts and kindnesses.

On the other hand, there are absolutely no sibling buffers. There are no brothers or sisters to divvy out the attention to, good or bad. Everything is focused on you. You either get all the praise or all the blame. There is no backup. It could be marvelous, or it could be terrible. All the hopes and dreams of your parents are suddenly focused on you. Sometimes it works out. Sometimes it doesn't. I would say that overall, it is a good thing. Some people say that being an only child automatically equates to evolving into a selfish, egotistical human who is unable to share anything, even living quarters, as an adult. I tend to think that I have turned out okay. I have had multiple roommates successfully, and I now even share a house with multiple daughters and a husband. I have an office filled with nine women at any one time. I think I have, in fact, learned to share. So, I turned out okay, I guess.

Chapter 6: The Santa Campaign

As a child, I would hold very long and persistent debates and diatribes about the existence of Santa Claus.

I believed for a very long time, up until the age of ten I think, which was way past the time of shattered childhood innocence of my peers.

I would argue in the most logical, geeky, economic sense you ever heard. My argument was that how could your parents possibly afford all those presents? It had to be Santa. There was just no other economic possibility. They would all look at me blankly and insist that he didn't exist. Finally, I got to realize it too. I finally broke down and asked my dad to give it to me straight and that I needed the truth! And then I cried and I think a piece of my childhood faded away at that very moment.

As an adult, I am still very much a fan of magic of all kinds and the idea of magic and Christmas wonderfulness. When I talk to my grandkids nowadays I speak more in terms of the belief in Santa. I tell them that there are a lot of things in life that we cannot see that are real, like the air we breathe and the germs that make us sick. I tell them that it is a matter of personal choice what they choose to believe in if it helps them have better faith in the world.

Chapter 7: Yes, my middle name is, in fact, a typo and yes, I do know how to pronounce my last name correctly.

My mother thought it would be a brilliant idea to spell my middle name as Alyce. This, of course, stood for Alice. This was the name she had lovingly copied from my Great Aunt Alice's birth certificate. She thought it was so unique and clever.

This, of course, caused me much distress and multiple failed spelling tests because every teacher was convinced that I still did not know how to spell my actual middle name correctly.

Finally, my mother came to my rescue and confirmed that my name was spelled correctly so I stopped failing spelling. That was a good thing.

However, she soon after learned that my Great Aunt Alice's (Yes, I said Alice, not Alyce) name was a typographical error on her birth certificate. My mother was horrified to learn that my name was not a brilliant twist but rather a comical mistake. I literally think she wanted to change it after that, but it was too late. I, however, felt vindicated that my spelling skills were no longer questioned. So, we left it at Alyce.

I have also spent a good deal of time having people correct me on the pronunciation of my last name, Katz.

Everyone wants to quickly jump to the conclusion that my real name is Laurie Katz (Pronounced Cats). You see, the a in America is a short, flat sound, whereas the a in Germany, where my people are from, is a longer ah sound. Also, the word Katz means cat.

So, much to everyone's disappointment my name is actually Laura Katz, not Laurie Cats. People have even gone to the persistence to inquire if I am really sure. I have literally been asked if I am sure about my own name. Who does that? All I have to say is, well, Mr. Smith (Smithe), I am, in fact, sure.

Chapter 8: Daddy's Little Daredevil

Once upon a time, when I was born, my dad had the greatest car ever. He actually had a gold 1967 Mustang fastback. The jewel of jewels. The vastly sought-after car to this day. This baby could shoot her way to 130 miles per hour in seconds.

He loved that car. I hear that I did, too, but I was too little to remember. He apparently loved to drive me around in that car to show it and me off to the world.

Well, one day, he took it too far, I guess. You see, back in the '60s and '70s, I-75 just kind of started at 12 miles, and off you went. So, it was a prime drag racing spot, as long as the police weren't watching. Well, one day, he apparently went racing along, this time with me in the car! I am told that I was smiling and laughing my baby's head off the whole time. Just to add to the fun, in those days, there was no common thing such as seatbelts or car seats or really anything significantly safe in any manner. So, there I was laughing hysterically, kind of constrained in this little net kind of thing in the semi-back seat of that car. No worries. Nothing happened, thank goodness. It must have been quite the thrill ride. However, he must have confessed to my mother at some point, and then it was bye-bye Mustang and on to some crappy used station wagon from my great aunt. Poor dad. I mean I guess he should have known better and kind of asked for it by confessing. If I had a picture of that car, I would show it to you, but I think it got lost in the shuffle somewhere. Just imagine a hard-to-find gold fastback beauty, and you get the point.

Chapter 9: The time my father shaved his beard

My dad had always had fantastic facial hair since my first memories of him. As a child, I loved to stroke it and, as a baby, pull on it while giggling my butt off. I thought it was the greatest thing ever.

Then, when I was a toddler, I think, he got the brilliant idea to shave it off, probably at the prompting of my mother.

I can remember him coming into my room to tuck me in, fresh after the shave. I immediately panicked and did not realize who he was and burst into tears. I thought my daddy had disappeared.

He talked to me calmly and allowed me to hear his voice. It then dawned on me that this stranger in front of me was actually my father. So, we hugged it out, and I tearfully requested that he grow it back and never do that again. He grew it back, and everything was eventually ok again and I could look at him without wondering who he was.

As an adult, I worry that that was my mother's idea for him to shave his beard. I worry that she was trying to find one more way to disturb the bond between my father and I. Although she had no reason to, I think she always felt a bit jealous about how close we were.

Chapter 10: The Cottage of my childhood

Some of the best memories that I have of my whole life are of the cottage. It was my great-grandmother's cottage on Trout Lake in Meredith, Michigan, near Houghton Lake. Actually, as it turns out, it was my great aunt's cottage, but that is a whole another story not worth telling. In my mind, it was my great-grandmother's cottage, and we will leave it at that.

That place was awesome. It was a real log house cottage with a big old fireplace with a large buck head over the fireplace. It was on the peninsula of the lake, so you had a lake in front, a channel on the side, and another lake in the back. Awesome!

It took over three hours to get there, but I would spend the entire time bursting with anticipation. I couldn't wait to see my grandma. I couldn't wait to see the cottage. I couldn't wait to see all the critters, fish, and wildlife.

I went exploring every single time we went there. Not like there was a lot to do in any of the neighboring towns so the cottage was the thing. I learned how to trap crawfish without getting pinched. My grandma used to show me how to "tease them" until that one time one almost snapped her finger off. Well, that stopped after that, so it was all about catch and release from that point on.

I might as well have been a boy for all the playing in the dirt and critter collecting that I did. I would collect whole buckets of snakes and frogs, sometimes at the same time, and then proudly go show them to my mother and father. My father thought it was awesome, of course, but my mother would just scream, grab the bucket from me, and insist that I go pour them out...outside the house, of course! Well, I did get a bit carried away at times. I can recall having up to ten or more snakes or frogs in my bucket. Don't worry. They all lived and were returned safely to the wild.

Fishing was awesome at the cottage. We had lots of perch and bass. I loved fishing with my dad. Sometimes, he would spend time trying to freak me out and act like I got him in the eye with the needle as I casted backwards. I didn't, of course, and we would laugh and move on.

I can remember the first time I learned to row the rowboat at the cottage. I had watched my dad do it for years, and then I finally decided to learn to do it on my own. So, began my rowboat tutorial. I got into the boat. My dad pushed us away from the shore and began the initial rowing. Then we practiced switching spots, so I was in the driver's seat when we got close to the channel area. I am sure he thought that we would be safer in the channel area because we would be closer to the shore in case I got into any trouble.

How wrong he was? I literally think that every animal in the lake and on the shores of the lake became in imminent danger in a second! Frogs and fish were literally bailing out of the lake onto the shore to escape the banging of my oars on said shore. No worries. All the fish were returned to the water safely, but eventually, my dad had to call it and take over. No animals were harmed in the process, thank goodness. And by the way, I did eventually learn to row a boat without issue.

There was a time that we actually almost drowned at the cottage, too. We were driving around in the old covered paddle boat. It had these big pontoons, an awning, and a steering wheel. When we pulled out, we failed to notice that there was a small hole in one of the pontoons. When we got through the channel to the back lake, the boat started rapidly sinking and turned over, trapping us underneath. We all had our fall clothes and heavy sweatshirts on, so we sunk immediately. I remember feeling weird, not anxious like everything was going to be ok. My dad was a great swimmer, and my mom found a way to drag me out and push me to the surface and we eventually swam our way to the back dock and got out of the water. After several hours by the fire and showering, we eventually warmed up. The paddle boat had to be dredged out of the bottom of the lake. Yes, we did end up getting it fixed in the end and using it again, now being more mindful of checking for holes BEFORE heading out. Remarkably, the cottage was such a nice place of peace that even that near-drowning incident did not dissuade us from our love of the place. I miss it even to this day. It got sold years and years ago.

Chapter 11: The Elementary School Years

So, I was in elementary school, two of them, in fact, from 1975 to 1982. We moved when I was in the third grade but didn't end up switching schools until the beginning of fourth grade for continuity's sake.

My first school, Starr Elementary I attended from Kindergarten through 3rd grade. It was an overall pretty good experience up through 2nd grade. I had teachers that were great and really believed in me. My second-grade teacher thought I was actually gifted and would be a good candidate for the gifted and talented program. However, my third-grade teacher did not have a lot of faith in me and didn't think that "I had what it takes" to be successful or an A student. She gave me a lot of 2s and 3s back when you graded that way. She had a lot of absences, and the class would absolutely go wild while she was gone. She was a real punishment fan. Everyone in the whole class would get punished for the actions of a very few. I would find myself stressing out and faking illness so I could go to the nurse's office and go home so that I technically would not be present for the punishment afterwards. This became a real habit for a while, I admit. Yep, I was afraid of her and became afraid of school. To add to the extra challenge, that was the year we finally realized that I couldn't see very well and was becoming nearsighted. That could have possibly explained some of the supposed poor performance. I'm just sayin. If I couldn't read it, I couldn't finish it.

Anyway, so after that I got some glasses. I had a really cute pair picked out, but no, my mom had other plans. She picked out these oversized tortoiseshell glasses that did not really fit my face at all, so there went the cute look I was striving for, and on came the geeky status. I mean. It was probably always there but now it was visual too.

Then, in mid-third grade, came the big move. We were still staying in Royal Oak, but instead of being in our nice multi-floor townhouse with several built-in playgrounds and next to a Baskin and Robbins, we opted for a broke down house closer to downtown that required over a month of repairs to be moved in ready. Being an only child with no consistent babysitters, I spent many a night in the back porch unfinished area watching inappropriate Saturday Night Live episodes from the 70s while waiting for my parents to finish working on the house. My mom still lives there to this day. Now, since Royal Oak is so fancy, the little box is apparently worth over 500,000. I am not buying it.

At the beginning of fourth grade, I relocated to a new elementary school call Longfellow Elementary after Henry Wadsworth Longfellow. It was a newer, renovated school. As a matter of fact, they were still in the middle of renovations when I started so I had to be bussed over to an old, now vacant elementary school, where my mother used to teach, called Grant Elementary. I had the most awesome toothless bus driver named George, who we gave great Christmas presents to, and my mom would be waiting for me at the bus stop with my pet guinea pig to great me when I came home. Yes, that's right. I said guinea pig. There were no traditional pets in my house. My dad was a seventh-grade science teacher at the time, so we had all the "unique pets" like Japanese quail, tarantulas, snakes, large fish, gerbils, and eventually guinea pigs.

As we slowly trended away from the spooky arachnids and reptiles and more toward guinea pigs, I started to have more friends who were willing to come over and play with my animals. I thought it was no big deal, but it, in fact true that not many kids want to come over and play with your tarantula. At one point, we had so many guinea pigs that we had up to twenty at a time. In fact, the first baby I ever delivered was a guinea pig. Maybe that's where my potential future love of obgyn started. Who knows?

Back in elementary school, I was now in the fourth grade. I now had a teacher who believed in me and actually helped get me into the gifted and talented program. Whoo! I was killing it! I also became a spelling bee champion up to the tri-school city-wide level, but my mom wouldn't let me go further than that. I regret that now because there could have been serious scholarships involved at the higher levels. No matter. I still have that to hang on to forever. Back when I was a contender.

By the time I got to 5th and 6th grade, a lot was changing. I had the same teacher for both grades, and he was really into the paddling. He actually had a paddle with holes in it! He like to demonstrate how it was just a flick of the wrist, and he could really paddle the heck out of you. Yes, back then, you could actually get away with that crap. Nowadays, you look at a kid sideways and get prosecuted. I am not really sure which direction is actually the better one.

5th grade is also the time that my body decided to develop boobs. I am always joking nowadays that I miss my 5th-grade C cups, but I actually do. Nowadays, those bygone C Cup days, while embarrassing and too big at the time, seem kind of dreamy compared to my ridiculous current Hs.

Chapter 12: The Tornado

Any of you out there remember the tornado that tore through Kalamazoo and Battle Creek in the 70s/80s? Well, I was there, baby!

It was initially a lovely spring afternoon, and I was at my cousin's band concert. The music was awesome. My cousin was awesome.

Then suddenly, the sky began to darken, and I hear my dad suddenly say.....huh. My head snapped to the right immediately. The fact that he made a comment about the sky meant that something truly messed up was about to happen. This is the man who stood outside, gazing at tornados just to scare all of us while we were hiding in the basement. I'll add with a smile on his face and no comments.

Well, the fact that he dared to say huh was a definite warning sign. So, I looked to the right, and the sky was green, and a funnel cloud was forming. Suddenly, the sirens went off, and the concert was stopped, and we all went racing for our cars.

We started the race home to my cousin's house with a car full....and got stopped by a train!..I am watching out the window as the funnel is stretching its way to the ground, and we are stopped by a train! With a line of cars behind us and nowhere to go! Oh crap!

Finally, the train passes and we can get going again. The funnel cloud is lazily taunting us and slowly reaching its way toward the ground, going back up and reaching down again.

We race toward town, and suddenly, my cousins decided they want ice cream. Mind you, the tornado has now reached the ground and is on its way. From afar, but still on its way.

Ice cream? Are you kidding me right now? So, my aunt and uncle stop at the ice cream shop under the guise of getting out of the weather, but I swear it was more about the ice cream.

We get in the ice cream shop and note all the tremendously big and heavy freezers around us and I have brief visions of possibly getting smushed by them, and they have no basement.

So, we change our minds and race toward their house while the tornado is plunging alone.

Thank the sweet lord we make it to their house and run for the basement and wait it out. We figure we will assess the damage later.

Thankfully, there was none for my cousins. And we were all still alive and well and uninjured, but sheesh! Was the potential possibility of ice cream worth possibly getting us killed?

Chapter 13: Family Gatherings

Traditionally we would have yearly family gatherings at Thanksgiving and Christmas. They were almost never at our house. They were usually at my grandmas, my cousins or my aunt's house on my mother's side. Sometimes, we would go to visit my father's side of the family, but not often. I think my mother disapproved of them, but I am not sure why. I sure loved to see them.

Every time a family gathering was coming up, I was initially very excited. I couldn't wait to see my family and visit with everyone. Soon, that excitement would change to worry and pre-anticipation. My mother would put a great deal of time and effort into making me worried that someone was going to mistreat her in some way and that I needed to be prepared to defend her.

As a child, you take this very seriously and you prepare during the whole car ride just what you would do or what you would say if anyone dared to be mean to your mommy. This made for a very intense and worrisome car ride.

Then, when we would get there, I never noticed anyone mistreating her in any way. The food was good. We had a good time. Nonetheless the pattern would repeat every family gathering time. It would always preemptively take away some of what should have been the joy of seeing family. But I always managed anyway.

Unfortunately, as I progressed into adulthood, due to a terrible misunderstanding, myself and my husband were disinvited from any future family gatherings. I found out much later in life that this was not really the intent. My family had just been barraged with so much false, horrible information from my mother about me that they didn't want to risk any public conflict for the sake of everyone else. As a result, I missed years and years of family gatherings due to this misunderstanding and my family did not get to meet or enjoy me, my husband, and my kids for years. Fortunately, this is all straightened out now, but so much time was wasted it makes me sad to this day.

Chapter 14: The First Time I Swore in Public

I can remember it clearly. Due to life in general at home, I developed a flair for swearing. Yep, all the big ones...the d word....the f-bombs....the whole thing. It would be all under my breath and not directly directed at anyone, but sometimes frustration brings you to new lows, and you say things you mean at the time but regret later.

Well, one day in sixth grade, nearly always surrounded by fellow swearers who should have already deposited millions in the swear jar, I was having a particularly bad day. I was waiting at the crosswalk and started to walk a fraction of a second before it was my turn, and the safety grabbed me. Without thinking, in the blink of an eye, I turned to him and loudly shouted, " Get your God Damn f...ing hands off me!"

Welp, that did it. I got reported immediately to the principal's office and it was a week of detention for me. The geeky prissy girl who never did anything wrong. Never mind that everyone was always swearing around me. I'm the one that was dumb enough to do it in front of someone that mattered. Lesson learned.

Chapter 15: Musical Protégé

When I was nine, my mother decided to enroll me in violin lessons. All of her friends had their kids in some kind of music lesson. She felt very behind. They had all been at it for years, and here was her sluncho kid not playing any instruments. Although I was clearly musically inclined and had already spent years giving spontaneous vocal performances of Delta Dawn, much to the delight of family friends.

So, I started violin lessons from a very talented, but cruel teacher. I was already years behind the others and reminded of it frequently. No worries, I caught on very quickly and, before you know it, became one of her personal tour monkeys as a demo student to garner more business. I started with the Suzuki method, so everything was learning by listening and then learn the music. There really was no sight-reading education involved. This was all fantastic up until sixth grade. I became a talented player but could not sight-read for crap.

I joined my first orchestra in sixth grade. I did very well at my audition and placed high up in the first violin section, but realized very quickly that I could barely sight-read the music and fell back quickly in the section. It was time for a change. I changed instructors and found a wonderful former Detroit Symphony Orchestra musician who helped me to catch up quite quickly in the sight-reading area, and I was able to catch up with my peers.

I played in a lot more orchestras through the years and loved every minute of it, to the point that I entertained the thought of becoming a professional musician. I won national music competitions even. I recorded performances of various concertos. The feeling of being on stage and performing pieces by memory and hearing the awesome applause at the end was a feeling that I will never forget. I actually was talented and I actually believed it. I even got into music school. My goal was to become a symphony musician. But, at the last minute, I realized that no position in a symphony would open up until someone moved or died, and how likely was that to happen? So, the practical part of me decided to go to regular college so I could make enough money to buy a grand instrument! Actually, in college, I auditioned and made it into the campus orchestra. In between my crazy busy schedule, I got invited to audition for the music school, which I politely declined and just kept playing for the enjoyment of it.

I still have a love of music that is strong and fierce and is present to this day. I still have the original violin that I purchased in the sixth grade for 650 dollars, which is now worth 8,000. I keep having to take breaks with all this cancer stuff, but then get back to playing as soon as I can.

Chapter 16: The year my family decided I was finally old enough that they did not have to hide their drug use

So, by the time I was twelve, I had heard years of rumors from my parents of the possibility of drug use and alcohol use by family members. I knew that my grandfather on my dad's side was a terrible drunk and died early of a massive stroke. I have vague memories of him that are actually good ones of me being in the car with him as he was yelling at my grandmother to go faster and I chimed in go! Loudly. I also have memories of him in a wheelchair after his stroke before he died.

I was also told that multiple members of my mother's family were alcoholics or used drugs, but the details were vague. Naturally, this also added to my anxiety before family gatherings because it had been fully engrained in me that drugs were evil and only evil people used them.

So, naturally, my anxiety about drugs and alcohol was at an all-time high, even by the age of 12. So, the year I turned 12, the Thanksgiving get-together was rapidly approaching. We went to the usual spot, my mother's cousin's house. This time, when dinner was done, the turkey was cleared off the table, and the drug paraphernalia came out. To me, who knew nothing, this looked like some very serious drug use going on. It was actually just marijuana pipes, and nowadays, that is legal anyway. But, to my 12-year-old mind, it was very serious and very scary. My relatives kindly informed me that I was now old enough that they did not need to hide in the bathroom anymore. I just needed to deal with it.

I was scared. I was mortified. I was ready to walk home....but I was in another state, did not have a big coat, and the weather was terrible. So, that wasn't happening. Then, my mother, who had set up my fear in the first place, made fun of me and acted like she had no idea why I was so concerned, so we stayed till the end anyway.

So now, as an adult, I know that there has been multiple kinds of drug and alcohol use, which has cost some lives in our family. For this reason, I have always been careful about my own alcohol use just because of my family history. Fortunately, I have been ok to this point.

Chapter 17: Middle School and High School

We are going to lump these together. Middle school was pretty awesome. I won more spelling bees, was in orchestra and choir, got to cut my hair for the first time, and actually start wearing makeup. Oh yes, and I got my first period, too. I was taking AP classes as well. A lot of change going on in Middle School.

In high school, I was the ultimate geek. I had these big ridiculous glasses and wore the Prairie girl shirts. I was in the orchestra but not allowed to join the choir with the more popular kids. I was friends with everybody. I judge no one. The brains, the geeks, the popular kids, and the burnouts were all my friends. I actually had kind of no idea just how much I meant to everyone at the time until much later at some class reunions. I did not have a lot of friends because I truly think that most of my classmates were not a fan of coming to my house to face my mother. No one actually wanted to or dared to invite me over or come to my house. I didn't really know why at the time. Now I know. No matter now. We have all reconnected as adults, so it is ok.

I can remember one of my most triumphant experiences in high school. I can remember the day I was in speech class, with a room full of burn outs, and I received the task of making a speech about how awesome classical music was. It was well known that I was a musician and violinist at the time and was a fan of classical music already. I almost wanted to faint at hearing this assignment. Turning a whole room of burnouts into classical music fans? It could not be done!

Not to be vexed. I sat down, took a breath, and came up with a plan. My plan involved this one essential element-----cartoons! In the early to mid-80s, the reruns of Bugs Bunny, Looney Tunes, and Tom and Jerry all used snippets of classical music in their cartoons. No problem! I just pointed out clips from said classical cartoons on my old VHS and pointed out the real names of the classical music being used and cha-ching! Instant classical music fans created. I am not sure that any one of them ever listened to a classical tune after that day, but I was pretty sure they had all watched What's Opera Doc? Or the Rabbit of Seville at one point in time. I got an A, of course.

I did well in high school, grade wise, and occasionally socially as well. I did have a core group of friends through all my classes and musical activities, so I did ok. I ended up third in my class due to two shlacky grades and the fact that classes weren't weighted, so my GPA was 3.999 something instead of 4.0. But U of M took me on anyway, and off I went.

The graduation was great. It was beautiful. Family came, but I still found myself being bummed out that I was only third in my class. I felt like I had let myself and my family down.

However, the honors and award ceremony before graduation was awesome! I practically wore a track in the aisleway with all the times I went to the stage to accept awards. I had plaques upon plaques and pins upon pins. It was amazing. All of them were things that had to be returned, but my name would be on them for the school forever. I know that sounds materially concentrated but I had worked very hard for all of them. I cradled them in my arms and took pictures with them that I have to this day. I was also feeling good because I finally got the bangs cut that I had wanted for years, so I thought I looked my best, too. That was a really good day!

Chapter 18: About those bangs

Remember how I said I finally got my bangs cut? Well, this had been a years-long battle with my mother. She was absolutely against it but couldn't exactly tell me why. At the age of 18, I somehow still felt like I had to ask her permission for everything.

Well, she finally relented, and I got my bangs cut. Again, the only real significant hair modification I had had in years. Well, she made darn sure, or at least tried to, make sure that I regretted it. She cried. She acted like she didn't even know who I was. She acted like she couldn't even look at me anymore. She even made a fuss about it and distracted my father from paying attention at his mother's own funeral! He finally had to stop her and bring her back to the reality of where we were at the moment before she would let the bang thing go. It hurt me, and I didn't care at the same time. I finally did one small thing that I wanted to do for myself that was not causing harm to anyone.

Chapter 19: On to U of M!

It was finally time for college. I am now realizing as an adult that I should have gone even farther away but I couldn't afford it. U of M looked like the place for me at the time, and they gave me a scholarship. I was off to be a famous lawyer and was going to study at the top political science department in the country at the time. I lived in a great dorm at East Quad, full of eccentrics, artists, and geeks. I felt right at home.

I started off well at college, getting good grades and succeeding where I needed to. Plus, I was a bit freer from my old home environment. The first two years were pretty good. I made some amazing friends, learned a ton of things, and even played in the campus orchestra on the side.

Then came my junior year, and things started crashing down. I had the opportunity to move out of the dorms and into a lovely apartment with my friends, which is what most students do. Unfortunately, these efforts were thwarted by my mother, and I was, let's say, urged strongly to move into a different female only dorm instead. This was the only way any funding from them would be continued. So, I did it of course, because I could not afford it on my own at the time with no prior warning to fund. I became isolated from my friends because they all moved on to living together, and we did not have the same classes anymore.

I started not completing work in my classes or at least procrastinating to the point that I had to withdraw to not fail.

The pressures from home continued even though I was far away, and I got depressed. I admit that I even thought about drastic measures to end this depression but, fortunately, did not follow through. I can remember standing on my balcony, wondering about what would happen if I jumped. Yes, I really got to that point. Fortunately, for whatever random reason, my phone rang, and I climbed down to answer it instead.

Of course, I was trembling and frightened after this. I tried to reach out to my mother about this but instead got yelled at instead. I got nowhere with this conversation. I was actually reaching out for help only to be told how dare I and be informed that she was not to be blamed for this. I wasn't trying to blame her. I was trying to tell my mother that I felt so depressed that I was not sure life was worth living. That was not the response I expected. But, also, fortunately, it made me realize that I had to take care of myself and that I was not going to give up my life because of her either.

Fortunately, my friends noticed this and reached out and I got help. I got strong again and finished college on a high note and on the way to a completely different track...medical school!

Chapter 20: Witchy Poos in the Family

I come from a long line of very interesting, very intelligent, and very messy women. When I say messy, I do not mean they don't know how to clean up for themselves, and I mean messy emotionally and in their relationships.

All the women on my mother's side of the family are tall, beautiful, fierce, fiercely intelligent, and terrible in their relationships. They all were on their way to great things and then got held up momentarily in some awful relationships and then were able to right themselves again. All except my mother. She ended up with my wonderful father, and I'm not sure how or that she ever got how wonderful he was in the first place. Yet he stayed by her side until his death.

I believe to this day that the women on my mom's side of the family are in possession of some very special gifts. I just don't think they all chose to use them in a positive way.

We all seem to be able to know intuitively when one of us is in some kind of trouble. The random phone calls start flying, and eventually, we discover that someone was currently in trouble or going through something. I think that is a good thing. It also makes them very good at tracking and figuring things out quickly. This part is a double-edged sword and one thing that has allowed my mother to stalk and track me, or at least attempt to, wherever I am, including my most recent hospital stay.

This is the negative part of the gifts. This is the part that has caused me a lot of fear and pain over the years. So, instead, I have chosen to use my gifts for good and help people exude good vibes and thoughts and reach out whenever I think someone is in trouble, not the creepy stalky part.

Chapter 21: Family Secrets

In my family, secrets were of the utmost importance to keep. It was my job to help my mother maintain the appearance of the perfect little family with the perfect daughter and the perfect blend of happiness and life in general.

I was never supposed to tell anyone what went on at our house. I was never supposed to let on that everything was not all bliss. We had the perfect family, and she was doing everything right....period!

For heaven's sake, her desire for control and pathologic co-dependency was to the extreme that we even had to dress alike for photos and events. No one could know the truth. Well, I knew the truth, and now, much later as an adult, the rest of my family knows as well.

Chapter 22: The Over Bundling

Yes, I was that kid, just like Ralphi's younger brother in A Christmas Story. I was the over-bundled kid. It did not matter how warm or cold it was. I was always the kid in some crazy snowsuit or oversized, super ugly coat. I am not really sure to this day what my mother was so concerned about.

I can even remember having to wear a Halloween costume over a snowsuit. Even into upper elementary school, I was the kid who always had to keep their coat on, even if it was 60-plus degrees outside. Every recess, I would stand sweating, watching all the other kids shed their coats and run and play with joy. And there was me, watching them wistfully, sweating all over, wishing I could take off mine too, but too afraid that my mother would find out. I even had teachers coming to me and offering to take it off for me and keep it a secret, but I would refuse. I just knew or thought I knew in my head that she would find out somehow and punish me. So, a lot of years of over-sweating and looking like a bundled dork on the playground went by. Finally, by the time junior high (middle school) came around, there was no more recess, so at least I didn't have to worry about that anymore.

Chapter 23: According to my mother, I am the reason she missed the opportunity to see my grandmother before she died

My beloved grandmother passed away of a massive heart attack. She presented to the hospital days before with chest pains and symptoms and was being monitored. My mother had the opportunity to go see her but did not. I was away with my boyfriend on break in the Upper Peninsula and did not know what was going on.

My grandmother ended up passing away from a massive heart attack that literally blew out the wall of her heart. My mother had not had the chance to go see her. I was travelling to get home, and there was no way to notify me of what was going on because there were no cell phones at the time.

As soon as I got home, my mother started screaming at me that It was because she was waiting for me that she missed the chance to see her mother before she died. I was only a young 20-something college kid at the time, so of course, I believed her. I learned later that she had the opportunity to see her mother but didn't. Nonetheless, the scars of that guilt persisted for a long time before I knew that. It was one of many of the things that I was blamed for over time.

In fact, I learned as an adult that my mother was constantly calling my relatives incessantly and telling them all of these made-up horrible things that I was supposedly doing. I knew none of this. My relatives actually became afraid to reach out to me because they were getting no input from me, so they believed what she was saying. In fact, she would campaign with relatives to have someone come and forcibly take me to a mental institution for my issues. Thank goodness that did not happen.

Chapter 24: I am not really sure how my mother got this way

I am told that once upon a time, my mother was a tall, beautiful, gracious woman with a bright smile that lit up any room. Over the years, she has evolved into a shriveled, hunched over, vengeful, pathologically co-dependent, abusive woman who is probably unhappy more days than not.

As a child and a young adult watching this change unfold, you try to figure out the reasons why. You are already being told that it is because of you and that you are the reason for every single day, every single bad mood, every single outburst, and every single bad outcome. So, you start believing it because you have finally heard the words enough. Your father keeps coming to you and begging you to understand that she is having a bad day and you need to help him fix it. You start over-striving and working your butt off in the hope of not disappointing her. You start believing that it really is all your fault.

Then, something finally happens. You finally get old enough to question it and stop punishing and doubting yourself. You start looking into everything she told you about her childhood. You ask her siblings about things and they have a completely different version of their childhood than the one she has given you. Then, you start to get it. Then things start to get really crazy. You see a therapist, and they basically advise you to run in the other direction because she is pathologically co-dependent on you, and things could become dangerous. But you can't do it because she is your mom. You feel like you owe her, and she makes sure to convince you of that regularly. Then, over time, little pieces of you get taken away more and more regularly until there is hardly any of you left.

Finally you get to the point that you can't take the poisonousness anymore as an adult and decide that your life will be healthier in general without her in it, as painful as that is.

And still, to this day, she persists in trying to be a part of it, seemingly innocent and helpless to the outside world and telling people that her horrible daughter will not have anything to do with her and that she prays for her everyday. When the real truth is that she preys on me every day.

Chapter 25: Hello, Wayne State University School of Medicine!

So, I started interviewing for medical schools after taking my MCATS. My main goal was to get into Wayne State University School of Medicine. I realized at the time that I would be attending school in Detroit of that time, which was basically a bombed-out hole and on the less safe side of safety. But, it was a place where I would have a multitude of hospitals to learn at, and it was a place that I felt would prepare me for anything and any kind of medical emergency. I was in!

Wonderful news! Wayne State accepted me early admission! I didn't even go to any other interviews because I was already overjoyed. I knew where I was going.

Medical school was grueling and amazing at the same time. There was a crap ton of information that had to be memorized in the first two years, most of which you would never use again, and then there was the blissful but also grueling clinical years for the next two years. These were the years when you actually got to rotate through the different specialties to attempt to guide you into your future decision-making process.

I struggled a lot for the first year of medical school and almost failed. I was still living at home. I had purposely tried for that not to be the case and investigated multiple apartment opportunities but my mother would conveniently get rid of the messages or not relay them, so I missed all those opportunities.

She had my dad build me a desk in my room for studying, but would constantly interrupt or would come running up and scream in my face in the night to disturb my sleep, so studying and being prepared for school was not easy.

But, the good news is I got smart and started making calls from school, retook classes over the summer, passed them all, and did get that apartment and my own loans to free me from her control.

Needless to say, things got a whole lot better. Classes were passed, and grades improved without the constant destructive distraction.

At first, I was sure I wanted to be an internist, but the hours of pontificating did not suit my personality, to say the least. I am a person of excitement and action, to say the least. Could I do internal medicine? Yes? Did I think I would enjoy doing it? No. Well, then, stop right there. Do not start off in a job that you are already questioning if you like. You will never do it well.

So, I went through my rotations and finally got to my Obgyn rotation. In my usual style, I picked the hardest, roughest, busiest rotation I could find at Hutzel Hospital. It was awesome! It was grueling! The hours were long! But it checked literally all the boxes. It had infinite variety. It was surgery, women's health, gynecologic oncology, ob, and gyn all in one! There were so many skills and brain requirements to be used every single day! And there were no men....except for circumcisions...lol, I literally cried at my first delivery because it was so wonderous and magical, despite the screaming and expletives. I mean, c'mon, you get it. It

really hurts for a minute or a hundred, man. I was
hooked, for sure.

Chapter 26: Yes, we really did have to walk that far

Remember the old Saturday Night Live skit with the old man who used to complain that he had to walk for miles with packs on his back in the snow? We all laughed and thought it was hilarious at the time. That's because we were watching that as adults.

Well, you know what? Some of that crap is actually true! From Kindergarten on, I had to walk about 2 miles to school.

(I actually mapped this out) back and forth, almost regardless of the weather. Yes, sometimes I got a ride but not a lot of the time.

I crossed crazy busy streets with no crossing guards. I grew up in the 70s when child abductions were at an all-time high, and we were still walking to school by ourselves, often with heavy backpacks but no bare feet, thank goodness. Back in the day, you had to live 4 miles or more away from the school before you qualified for bussing. Nowadays, it seems like even kids who live multiple blocks away can be bussed. I am not saying it's a good thing that we had to walk so far at so young of ages, but for heaven's sake, these kids of today could use just a little toughening up.

Chapter 27: My grandmother was a fantastic woman. I think she just forgot for a moment

My grandmother died of a massive heart attack early in her 60s. It was way too early. She had a ton left to live and to give, but I think she just forgot how wonderful and full of potential she was.

Once upon a time, before marrying her high school sweetheart and getting pregnant, she was fierce, intelligent, a model and exuded radiance on the daily. I have seen the pictures to prove it. I have heard the stories, too. She was the prom queen and the most popular girl in school.

Once the babies started coming and, the relationships started to fail and the marriages accumulated, three in total, I think she lost confidence in herself. I think she blamed herself for falling in love with the wrong person or her constant search for someone to provide for her and for her children, forgetting about her own feelings and need for real, true love and respect.

Even after multiple children and failed marriages, she was still amazing in my mind. She was smart, still gorgeous, could whistle better than Bing Crosby, and was a tall goddess. She told me how she used to get in trouble for whistling because her mother told her it was not ladylike. That, of course, only made me want to listen to her whistle more. Every Thanksgiving was a giant whistle fest, along with a ton of good food. I couldn't wait to see her each time. She even had a lulling Lauren Bacall-style voice that just soothed me. I thought she was fantastic.

As I mentioned in a future chapter, as her happiness declined, so did her health. She developed obesity, heart disease, and diabetes. I think she just stopped taking care of herself, so we lost her early. It was a terrible waste. I always thought it was such a bonus to have such a young grandmother who would be around for a long time. It was not to be, however. My great aunt told me after grandmother died that she saw her in a dream, youthful as in the past, smiling ear to ear. My plan is to hold onto that thought and the hope that she is now finally happy.

Chapter 28: That time, we worked in Jamaica

My future husband/boyfriend at the time started getting big ideas by the time our 4th year of medical school rolled around. We decided we needed to broaden our horizons. We decided that we needed some worldly experience.

We got the brilliant idea to go work in Jamaica for a month or so. We had heard how beautiful it was. We were imagining palm trees, the seven-mile beach, snorkeling and beautiful mountain and ocean scenery.

Well, we got some of that on our weekends off. We also experienced some amazing food and culture as well.

The rest of the time, we experienced crime, extreme poverty, and tons of areas still in desperate need of repair since the hurricane ten years before. We received judgement for our unmarried status while having to treat significant levels of rampant STDs.

We dug in our heels and scaled fern gully to treat a woman with a huge abscess being cleansed by maggots. We took care of pregnant women using only old-school fetoscopes pressed against our foreheads to try to hear the fetal heartbeat. We traveled by pickup truck to remote clinics where a fancy doctor would fly in on a single-engine aircraft and drop off a single box of meds, wish us good luck on working with what he left, and then promptly leave us to just figure stuff out.

The stress was incredible, but so was the learning. We craved the weekends to go and explore and manage to find just one credit card with some remaining money on it to use for expenses. We almost didn't make it off the island because we didn't realize there was a departure tax that could only be paid in jamaican, and no one wanted to exchange our American dollars.

Having said all that about the stressful moments. There were beautiful moments, too. We realized that everyone who told us about the beauty of Jamaica had not actually seen the real Jamaica. They were just on some all-inclusive resort somewhere.

Some of the scenery was breathtakingly beautiful. The swimming was amazing. The ocean and the sunsets were gorgeous. Some of the people showed a type of kindness that I had never before seen. The food was awesome. I am still glad that we did it.

Chapter 29: I found a man!

Did I forget to mention the other awesome thing about medical school? I found my future husband there! Lemme paint ya a picture. I was fresh off a near engagement first year of medical school. I mean, like, I knew the guy was probably about to propose, and I knew it was not going to work out, so I did not want to be the girl to let that guy down, so I ended the relationship before that happened. I still cared very much about him, but we were definitely headed in totally separate directions.

Then, I met my future husband. Believe you mean I had no preconceptions of this notion. This guy was the one that laughed exactly 30 seconds longer than anyone else in the entire auditorium at literally...everything! He also rocked the 70s leisure suits to class. No kidding. The first and most favorite gift I gave to him was this 1972 brown and orange plaid Pierre Cardin jacket. I cannot make this up.

So, one day, the guy I am currently sleeping with expressed no interest in attending a concert my roommate and I were going to. In pops in this guy who invites himself along to the concert. We go to pick him up at his house in a semi-scary area of Detroit. He is dressed in a mock turtle neck with a Nehru jacket. We go to the concert. He pays attention with rapt attention. He asks questions. He listens to what I say. I am intrigued. We all decided to go dancing in Detroit but cannot find a good place to stay. So, we say that we are going to head all the way up to Royal Oak to a different place, and he offers to follow us up there! Once we get there, I realize that he likes to dance and has the whole place heying and hoing in like 20 minutes. Then, he waits outside the bathroom for me and compliments my hair and my literally 90s horrific outfit! Whaaat? This one may be a keeper, ladies! Then he offers to drive me home, gives me one kiss that has me floating for days, and we talk until dawn. Yep, we are still together today, legally married for 25 years and this night was January of 1993.

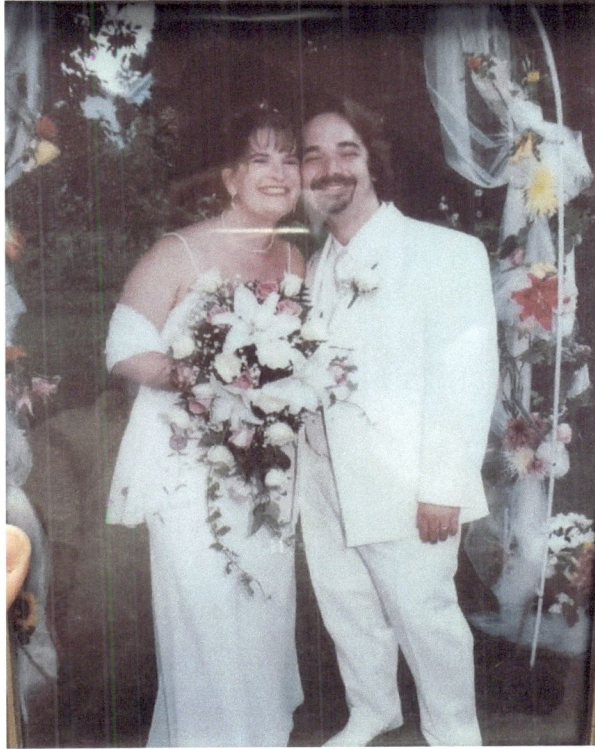

I can remember the exact day the thought of marrying him actually popped into my head. We were not even engaged yet. We were both still in residency….in different states. We were wandering through a store at a mall that was close to my apartment. It doesn't even exist anymore. It was called the Lion Store. There was a random beautiful white dress with a purple sprig of flowers on it. I heard him murmur under his breath…boy, I could see myself marrying you in that. I'm sure he thought I didn't hear him, but I did. I went back later and bought that dress and hung it in my closet for a rainy day.

Well, 2 years later, that sunny, beautiful day came, and we got married at the courthouse in front of the magistrate, who looked remarkably like Lanie

Kazan. Then, we took fake pictures in front of the local Presbyterian church.

Then, everyone had a fit so we had a big party and got married again 6 months later, wearing that very dress and he wore a white tuxedo, in our own back yard. We had a beautiful tent, chandeliers, and a black and white checkered floor. Thank god we put up the tent two days before because a tornado tore through town. It was still standing and now the ground was not soaking wet.

We had an arch created by our own guests, each contributing a flower to it. We wrote our own vows and our friends stood up and did readings for us. We pulled out a Victrola and danced to Always by Guy Lombardo. It was magical

Chapter 30: BTW he has a child already….Long distance relationships are tough.

Did I mention previously that my medical school boyfriend/future husband had a child already? Well, neither did he at first. I found that out about a month in but, too late, I was already locked in. I was in love for sure and not going anywhere and immediately fell in love with his daughter too.

So, my boyfriend and I were both in medical school at the same time, and we lived over 50 miles apart. He was living at home with his daughter, and I was living over 50 miles away in Madison Heights, a solid 50-minute drive away. Was it tough? Yes. Did we make it work get through medical school and raise a toddler together in the process? Yes. We weren't alone of course. His parents were there to help plus other helpers along the way. We were very lucky.

I am sure that there was more than one time when we were probably too tired to drive, but did it anyway just to carve out time to see each other outside of class. We also took the time to do medical missions in other countries while making sure that his daughter was well cared for. We definitely made the most of our situation. I would not recommend trying to raise a toddler and going to medical school, but we did it and I don't regret a thing.

We made it through, had an amazing graduation at the Detroit Opera House, and were ready to go off to residency!

Chapter 31: All the car rides

I spent years of my life riding in the car with my father. Each of these rides was not for fun. They were rides to try to offer me a temporary rescue from the abuse from my mother, either physically or emotionally. They were rides to try to talk me down and get me to understand why she is how she is. They were rides to try to convince me that she really did love me but just didn't know how to show it.

They were exhausting. They did me no good. They did not resolve the issues or solve anything. I think they were his attempt to try to fix something that was not fixable. To be honest, he had actually tried to stand up for me in the past but had failed so miserably that he never tried again. I understood. I didn't blame him. He loved my mother despite all of her faults. He loved me, too. I couldn't ask him to choose between us, although I secretly wished he would.

These rides continued for years until the point that I cut off contact with them both.

Chapter 32: On to Residency!

We are not going to talk about this part a lot since I have already gone over it in a previous book. But, just to refresh. Residency is the next step after medical school. It is an extra 3 to 7-year program after completing your MD or DO degree from medical school so that you can pursue a career in a particular specialty. And no, a physician's assistant or a nurse practitioner is not the same thing as a doctor. They are amazing as well, but have different training for different adjunctive purposes.

My choice was obgyn, as I previously stated. I went to the Medical College of Ohio for residency. It was a fantastic choice. I got a full even breadth of all things obgyn, gyn oncology, family practice, emergency medicine, and even internal medicine. You see, at my time of training, obgyns had been temporarily reclassified as primary care, so I got the benefit of all that extra training, which I still use to this day. The four years were, once again, grueling but worth every minute, and I truly felt prepared to deal with anything when I was done.

I feel the need to refresh everyone for a minute that residency in my day is not what it is now. I had no restricted hours or set lecture reserve times. I was sometimes up for 36 or more hours at a time and still expected to work. I am not saying that is a good thing or the safest thing. But, as a long-time independent, non-employed physician responsible for everything on my own, by my own, it definitely prepared me for the reality of what I was about to take on. I get concerned sometimes that the residents nowadays are not as prepared for real life as I was. I am very glad that more thought has gone into the preservation of their health and mental health, but I am not always sure it coincides with reality. Being a doctor, whether you are employed or not, is a full-time all the time job in which you need to have the want to care for patients completely throughout their whole course. It is not really meant to be a 9 to 5 er with a set cut-off time for responsibility.

Chapter 33: Well, but I AM Mrs. Pasko in public, but I am Dr. Katz professionally

Ok, so here's the deal. The man took what felt like forever to marry me. I mean totally worth the wait, but it felt like forever. Granted, we were a tad busy trying to raise a kid, finish medical school, and finish residency.

Yes, I get it. A lot was going on. Not a lot of time for weddings etc. I mean, I already knew I loved him and was in it forever for years anyway, piece of paper notwithstanding.

So, by the time we finally got married, all the doctor's paperwork was already set. The titles were already in place. Patients already knew me as Dr. Katz. It would have cost a lot to change every piece of paper, every license, and completely change my practice name. Plus, where I lived, you couldn't swing a dead cat and not hit someone who either was a Pasko, knew a Pasko, was also a Dr Pasko, or went to school with one. It was a kind of a done deal. Don't worry. My husband jokes every day that I didn't take his name because I am ashamed of him. That's not true of course..lol It really was about the paperwork. Our love is real and meant to last.

Chapter 34: Private Practice

I have been in private practice since 2000. Initially, I was in an employed group practice that just didn't work out, and that's fine. It got me a year and a half off in between the group practice and starting my solo practice and allowed me the time to be a stay-at-home mom with my baby girl! We explored everything. We bonded. We went everywhere. I am not sure she has recovered from the future separation since...lol.

After a year and a half of being poor and being at home, and my restriction of the covenant was over, I decided it was time to get back to work. I decided to apply for a position and privileges at my local hospital. Apparently, they were not ready for a female, Caucasian, English-as-a-first-language female obgyn in town. Well, I took the worst deal ever and set myself up as an independent physician in a used office anyway. It was tough. I didn't have enough money to even really get started but I did it anyway!

I have been in an independent solo obgyn practice since August 2002, and I haven't looked back.

Once again, the hours have been grueling at times, and the extra in-house on-call was really tough. I am responsible for everything I do 24 hours a day and 7 days a week. I have to get permission or coverage every time I even want to go to the bathroom out of town. Eh. It is what it is. But, you know what I love about it? I get to decide on and determine the quality of care all the time, every time. I have a much better chance of securing a positive outcome for the patient if I keep myself the one in charge. The other side of that coin is that there is no guaranteed salary or funding and everything is all up to me. Hiring and firing employees, paying said employees, office expenses, insurance, overhead...all mine. It is a whole lot, but omg so worth it. Despite all the struggles and responsibility, I wouldn't change a thing. I love what I do and I want to do it for as long as I can.

Chapter 35: The first baby is on the way. Of course, I have to do it rare and complicated

It's November of 2000. I find out just after a nice Thanksgiving celebration with lots of wine that I am pregnant! We are so excited we can't stand it. I am doing good, and then about 6 weeks in, I start having pain on my right side. I call my doctor's office, and they tell me to go to the er. I get examined, and they say they can see a cyst on the opposite side of us but can't see the baby yet, but it's very early, so not to worry. It's probably just referred to as pain because of the cyst.

So, I wait it out. I keep having more pain, but I remember what the doctor said and tough it out. Well, one day, I couldn't tough it out anymore. It hurt too much. My husband took me back to the ER. The ER physicians looked me over. No obgyn physician came to see me. I asked for an ultrasound. During the usn, the technician says she does not see anything, and she is going to advised the doctor to proceed with a d and c. I look quickly out of the corner of my eye and see what I think is a heartbeat actually in the uterus. I quickly inform the technician who says that I am incorrect. Mind you, I am already a practicing obgyn at this point, so I know what I am looking at. She tells me again that I am incorrect, so I literally had to grab the probe that was inserted vaginally and scan myself, visualizing the embryo very much alive in the uterus. She almost seemed upset. I then scanned my right side where the pain was, and there was a large cystic structure that looked like an ectopic pregnancy as well. Once again, the technician got angry with me and stopped the exam. I was then sent to the er, and they were about to send me home, and still no obgyn had seen me. I refused to go home, and I refused to let them see the live fetus out of me. Instead, I called my friend, who was a general surgeon and asked if he would come see me because the pain was getting worse and I knew something was happening.

Thank goodness he came. He took one look at me and rushed me to the OR, thinking it was my appendix. They tried to use spinal anesthesia for the baby's sake, but as soon as he entered my abdomen, he discovered that it was full of blood, so they had to put me immediately under general anesthesia anyway.

I woke up later to be told that I did actually have a ruptured ectopic pregnancy that was actively rupturing at the time of surgery. Thankfully, they did not touch the fetus inside the uterus, and we just crossed our fingers, and I went home a few days later.

The obgyn that was called to see me did appear in the or for a few minutes before they put me to sleep, never saw me in the hospital, and then called me days after discharge, telling me that I must have been right after all.

Thank god I did not allow them to send me home. If I would have ruptured while my husband was driving on the highway, what could he have done? I would have died and not be here right now.

Needless to say, I did not go back to that obgyn. I did go back for follow-up to my original obgyn for the remainder of the pregnancy though, and ended up with a healthy baby girl thank the lord. She is still here and feisty to this day.

Chapter 36: The second pregnancy was feisty as well

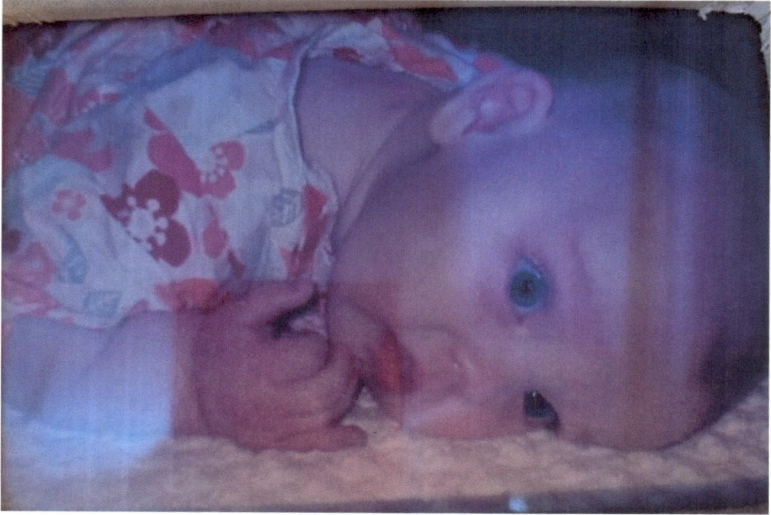

I got pregnant again in 2003 after an early miscarriage. This pregnancy overall went well. No preeclampsia this time just gestational diabetes, which was manageable with glyburide and insulin.

I was technically a possible vaginal birth after c-section candidate, but I decided to go with the c-section to be on the safer side, hopefully with prior planning.

However, me being me, nothing goes according to plan. Instead, I decided to go into labor during a very difficult hysterectomy that I was performing when I was 36 weeks pregnant. The patient had failed to notify me that she had a history of extensive radiation treatment after her previous colon cancer. I thought it was going to be an easy abdominal hyst, so I booked it. Well, whaddya know, I started having contractions right in the middle of it, when the patient was already open, and I had already realized that she was full of adhesions and it was going to take a long time.

So, me being stubborn, I puffed quietly under my mask, and my surgical assistant surgeon was none the wiser. Luckily, we made it to the end of the surgery and I casually asked my assistant if he could do the orders, then snuck upstairs to have a baby!

When I got upstairs, I was contracting away. My office manager at the time caught me trying to monitor myself and sent me to labor and delivery. They hooked me right up. My husband was out of town, and so was my obgyn. I was still contracting away and couldn't help pondering the thought that I was at risk for uterine rupture because of the previous c-section. My husband arrived and nervously asked if I could just get a shot and stop this labor. I giggled at him and said no, the baby was trying to tell me something. We were going to let this proceed.

When all was said and done, I had a health, almost 7-pound baby girl 4 weeks early with the cord wrapped around her neck twice and her torso. She knew what she was doing, trying to get out. She, too, is alive and well today.

Chapter 37: Pets

I never really had traditional pets as a child. I was always told that I was allergic to cats and dogs and anything usual. Plus, my dad was always busy bringing home all the unusual and creepy pets like gerbils, tarantulas, snakes, quail, and fish of different kids. You know, the kinds that no one but me wanted to play with.

Well, as an adult, I decided to get curious and recheck all my allergies and go through and actually complete the allergy shot regimen.

Lo and behold, I ended up successfully treating my allergies and ended up not being allergic to cats or dogs. It was time to get some.

First, we started with Puss, our first cat and normal pet. He was really more like a dog than a cat. he came when you called him. He actually likes to snuggle. He "talked to you." He was wild about flies to the point that he got so excited about the possibility of eating them that he could only make chirpy and gibberish noises.

We originally headed to the humane society to pick up this big, fearsome, grey cat named Natasha. We were all psyched up and ready to go. Well apparently, Natasha was having a bad day that day. She wanted nothing to do with us. She hissed and scratched. Being newbies, we were terrified of course, but feeling guilty about backing out.

Then, as if on cue, we look over and see one of the helpers holding baby Puss. He was just snuggling on her shoulder. He was already tested and feline negative, and because he was an owner, surrender was available for adoption.

Score! We took him, and the rest was history. Best cat on the planet.

Then came Starla, our next cat. A cute little black stray with one white splotch on her paw, a hint to her probably Siamese blend heritage.

We got Starla as a stray at a car show. I had brought my father and my five-year-old to a car show. There was a cute kitty that they wanted to pet. She was sitting on someone's lap.

Mind you, at the time, my father was begging to suffer the effects of multi-infarct dementia, so it was like having two 5-year-olds with me at the car show.

So, they went to pet the kitty, and lo and behold, she turned out to be a stray who needed a home and had actually burned her paw while peering into a muffler on a car.

You might as well have printed a sucker stamp on my forehead. Both my addled father and my five-year-old came to me immediately, explaining the urgency of rescuing Starla.

So, home she came, of course. We originally intended her to be trained to be a kitty at the local nursing home where my father was going to go, but we fell in love with her anyway so she stayed with us.

The next pet in line was Charlie. We decided that we had our crap together with the cats, so why not try a dog? We also wanted to make sure that we got a rescued one to ensure a maximal challenge apparently.

So, we went to the humane society. We looked at a bunch of dogs, but none really fit the bill. Then, they brought out Charlie or Chompers, as his name was at the time. I should have taken this as an initial hint of his true nature. Lesson learned.

So, they brought out this cute little bedraggled Shih Tzu out to meet us. For us, he rolled on his back to have his belly pet, and he gently sniffed my husband's ear.

Needless to say, we were sold. We arranged to take him home. My daughters, my mother-in-law, and the babysitter went with me to pick him up. We had not yet picked up his supplies because we thought it would be an awesome idea for him to pick them out himself. Genius!

So, we get there and they have him all ready for us and already in a harness that we get to keep! Score!

They were even willing to put him in the car for us! Another score! They also said that they would not make us sign the usual contract and that returning him would be ok as long as we got another dog.

Still not picking up on the cues, we thought we scored again, and they put him in the back of the car for us.

So, we headed off to PetSmart. He seemed content in the back of the car. We let him out of the car and headed for the door to PetSmart.

As soon as he saw that automatic door open, it was as if the Tasmanian Devil himself had appeared and transformed Charlie into a snarling tornado demon. He snarled, frothed, spun.

I had to take a stunned second. I quickly grabbed my little daughter's hand away as she was trying to comfort him.

I told everybody to go back to the car and start it up with the air on. I was going to sit with the dog on the super-hot pavement until he calmed down. I had read a whole book on dog behavior and I was sure I had this handled.

So, after 25 minutes or so of sitting on the boiling hot pavement and multiple concerned passers-by inquiring how we were doing, he finally stood up and, tilted his head, and regarded me. It's like he finally realized that I was not going to do him any harm. He had no reference before this to believe that would ever be true. He had only known abuse and suffering and had apparently been returned two other times before we took him.

So, I managed to get him up and back to the car. I was too exhausted to be able to realize that I could have simply lifted him up by his harness to put him in the car. Instead, I called the babysitter to hold his leash because I was going to run into the store and get his stuff anyway! In the meantime, members of the Michigan Humane Society were visiting the store and looking outside, wondering why the poor animal was out in the heat.

Oh lord, I started yelling from the cashier line don't touch him. I will be right there. In the meantime, my babysitter had the brilliant idea to put a crate so he could hop into the car.

I came flying out of the store, and we flung his stuff into the car, and off we went.

Despite all the chicanery in the beginning. After a ton of work and, training and love. I am telling you that dog evolved into the absolute best dog on the planet. Taking care of him and giving him the life, he deserved is literally one of the best things we have ever done.

Chapter 38: The garbage bag of hate letters

After many years of family isolation, an aunt of mine suddenly reached out. She had finally decided to find out if everything was mother was saying about me was actually true.

Well, first of all I was stunned that a family member reached out. Second of all, I needed to inform her that I had no idea what she was talking about. Apparently, in all our years of separation, my mother had been telling the family all kinds of terrible, albeit made-up, things about me to keep them from contacting me and keep them from inviting me to family things.

I politely informed my aunt that none of them were true. I instead enlightened her on all the terrible things my mother had done and that she had been sending me terrible letters, fake death certificates for my father, etc., over the years, so I had no contact with her.

Needless to say, my poor aunt was shocked. She asked to see the letters because apparently, she had been forewarned that I might make up a story like this. I happily handed over to her the years of hate mail and fake death certificates I had received from my mother over the years. She would even send me a fake death certificate for my father for my birthday right to my office. I would find myself calling multiple relatives, asking if my father was actually dead.

My aunt still has that garbage bag of hate to this day. She keeps it in case I ever foolishly consider letting my mother back into my life. No. I don't want to see them again, but it's somehow still good to know that proof is out there.

Chapter 39: My father died

My mother used to use my father as the ultimate final playing card if you well. She realized after I cut off contact with them that I actually cared deeply for my father. But I knew that I could not keep in contact with him without actually being in contact with her.

As he began to suffer from multi-infarct dementia, he began to have to rely more heavily on her. She would try to use this to reinvolve me in her life, but I still held off. The abuse and trauma was just too much.

It is true. I wasted the last few years I could have been in my father's life. I just couldn't do it.

In 2008, my father passed away. After years of abuse by my mother and failed attempts by my father to intervene, I stopped having contact with them. He developed dementia and aphasia in the meantime, and she continued to try to contact me to warn me about my last chances to see him. She ended up taking me to court for guardianship of him which I had not actually applied for.

I had gone to pick him up during one of her many hospitalizations because I knew he was unable to care for himself. When he stayed with me, he blossomed. He began to read again. He started exercising again. We found a way to communicate effectively with a combination of words and hand signals and got along quite well. With my mother's extended hospitalization and a few accidents at my house, I thought it was safer to have him at a nursing facility in the meantime.

Unfortunately, my mother did not like that idea at all and checked herself out of the hospital and recruited my aunts to come and literally kidnap him out of the nursing home, almost running over one of the nursing home employees in the meantime. Sadly, he was gone /passed away within 6 months of that kidnapping and after the court date.

He passed a massive brain hemorrhage at the hospital after being there for several days. She never let me know he was even there. She had a relative call me minutes after he died instead and had convinced the doctors and staff that she begged me to come for days when I did not know he was even there. I was literally calling the hospital trying to find out what happened to him, and they were yelling at me for not coming.

When I took a breath and explained to them that I did not know that he was even there, they were shocked. This seemingly frail little old lady had told them that she begged me to come. This, unfortunately was not a new scenario for me. This is the kind of thing she had been doing to me my whole life. I decided I finally had enough. That was the last straw.

Chapter 40: The Funeral

I found out in a roundabout way about my father's funeral. It was going to be at a beautiful church, and he was to be cremated, and it was going to be postponed until a significant period of time after his death. I was torn about what to do with this information. I was afraid of how things would go. I eventually got up the nerve to decide to attend, even if I wasn't invited.

Before the day of the funeral, I spent weeks gathering old photos and putting together a very special scrapbook for my father. I vowed to myself to attend and sit quietly and not cause any trouble and try my best to keep myself together.

On the day of the funeral, my mother actually had guards at the funeral in case I "tried something." Umm what? Try something. It's horrible and laughable. At the same time, to even think of it.

After the funeral was over I quietly went into the meeting hall and just sat down with my scrapbook, looking at my pictures and not speaking to anybody.

Instead, an amazing thing happened. All my dad's old friends and colleagues came up to me and were visiting with me checking on me and sharing stories about my father. It was so good to see them all again. My mother, of course was not pleased and indicated to have me leave. No worries. I accomplished what I needed to do.

Chapter 41: I was a dance mom, a cheer mom, an orchestra mom, a band mom, and a sports mom!

Yes, my kids participated in a ton of things and I was happy to go along with it.

I was a mom of girls only, and they were very involved. It was a lot of driving, a lot of prep, and a lot of cheering your head off. I loved every minute.

I tried my best to make every concert, every performance, every recital, and every game, despite whatever was going on, no matter how many women were in labor and no matter how busy my surgery schedule was. I am happy to say that I actually did manage to make the most of it. This was not typical parent behavior of most of my colleagues at the time. To me, those kids and my family were and are the most important people in my life. I love my career and love using my brain to help people each and every day. But, family first is a rule that I still follow even now.

What's interesting, though is that I didn't seem to fit any of the mom stereotypes of the activities at hand.

Most of these moms were gorgeous and always dressed up to the teeth at every event. I was impressed. There was no way I could look that good for the 6 am call times. Even the sports moms seemed to clean up nicely for the sporting events.

Well, more power to them I say. I usually would come dragging in after a full night of call, still wearing my scrubs after saving lives and still cheering my head off and trying to fit in. But I made it on time, dang it! That has to stand for something!

I loved it, but I found myself wondering at times, was there a competition off and on the stage or field at the same time? Wasn't this about our kids, not us? I am all for bragging, etc. but ultimately, it is supposed to be about the kids.

Don't get me wrong. I have met some fantastic freaking power moms along the way. I am just not sure that all of them were able to keep in mind that this was supposed to be for the kids.

Chapter 42: The cottage I always dreamed of

For years we dreamed as a family of owning our own cottage. Not a lakeside mansion, not a second home, just a cottage. Even a ramshackle shack would do.

I spent like 5 years watching every real estate website, including one called Great Cottages.com, which I don't think even exists anymore. I dragged my small children to multiple showings all over the state. My husband was not ready to go along until the hunt was more than browsing.

Finally, after years of watching, I finally found a local realtor in the Irish Hills that had been doing it for decades and was actually a local and knew everything about real estate and the community.

I figured the Irish hills was the place to be. All those car executives had to be on to something. I looked at a lot of huge and beautiful and expensive places. I was not interested. Then suddenly, the bubble popped in the economy and the prices went down. At the same time, this adorable tiny 850+ square foot shack on the hill popped up on the Great Cottages website. It was on a lake that seemed very familiar. As it turns out, it was right across the lake from friends of ours that we had known for years. I spent years listening to them talking about how wonderful it was.

I called my friend to check. Her first words were I KNOW THAT PLACE! I can see it in the window with my binoculars! Umm what? I was not sure at the time that that was an actual selling point.

Needless to say, we took a chance and took a look. It was fresh out, the 50s perfect. Up on a hill so flood risk was low. Had a beachfront. Clear lake, you could see your hands and feet in at all times, so no potential complaints from the kiddos. Natural spring-fed lake. Small and adorable, with a four-season room out the back.

Umm...mine? Please? Thank the lord, my faith in realtors was restored. Our realtor was actually our agent and the seller's agent at the same time. The whole process, despite a multitude of steps, took only one month. Record time by my standards. We were moved in by Memorial Day.

This place has been a spot of heaven since the day we bought it. No matter what is going on or how bad anyone's attitude is on any given day, as soon as we get in the car to head there, everything is better. I am convinced it holds some kind of magic. Everybody always asks us why we didn't get something bigger. Well, one, we couldn't afford it, and two, we didn't want it. As I said before, I didn't need a second house. I wanted something that I could clean without even unplugging the vacuum in 30 minutes or less. It checked all the boxes and still does.

Chapter 43: I got the bright idea to start an aesthetics business and then Covid hit

I had already been in business for over 18 years. Things were going well. I started seeing a number of patients that were going to spas and salons and having injuries, complications, and lack of success with their procedures. I spent a lot of time fixing and repairing mistakes. Finally, I thought, why am I not doing these things myself in a safe and affordable medical environment?

I started first with laser hair removal. This went great for a few years, so I decided to expand with CoolSculpting and Morpheus8. These are permanent fat freezing and radiofrequency microneedling procedures. The same that are offered in Hollywood and other famous places but for far less the price.

So, of course, as soon as I financed those purchases, Covid hit, and those kinds of procedures were deemed unessential, and I wasn't even able to use the machines. I sure had to still pay for them though. So, that put a little bit of a crapper on the possible profits of those things, but I did not give up!

Chapter 44: Hodgkin's Lymphoma

I already wrote a different book about this so we are not going to spend too much time on this. Suffice it to say that apparently, the stress of the Covid pandemic was not enough, and the universe decided to throw me another curveball in the form of Hodgkin's lymphoma.

This was awful and scary news but, thankfully, very treatable without patient chemotherapy. It was exhausting. It was a completely different health experience than I've ever had before, but I made it through and are still continuing with follow-up.

Chapter 45: My husband had emergency open heart surgery

I was barely done with my chemo from my first cancer. We hadn't been on a vacation in a long time. I was recovering from my dead thyroid from chemo with little to no energy. I felt pent up and was determined to go on this long-planned vacation. It had been more than long enough.

I can remember when my husband walked into the house after fertilizing the lawn with a weird look on his face.

I actually got immediately angry and started yelling at him that there was no way we weren't going on this vacation and that we deserved it, damn it!

He then looked down quietly and said that he was sorry, but he was having chest pain.

Whaaat?! Chest pain! Of course, I immediately apologized and changed course, and we took him straight to the ER. His EKG had some minor abnormalities but we knew something was going on for the pain he was having.

Fortunately, I used my connections to reach out to the cardiologist right away and my husband got a cath the next day. His vessels looked awful with multiple blockages, and they looked like rats had chewed on them. We were told that he was not a candidate for a stent and actually needed open heart surgery.

Oh my god open heart surgery! I had to follow him by car while he went by ambulance to another hospital.

He was in a lot of discomfort, and all the nitro in the world wasn't helping. They were going to wait to do his surgery. I wouldn't take no for an answer, and he got his surgery earlier than planned. I was determined not to lose him. I was not going to let that happen.

His surgery went well. It was extensive and scary, and he required multiple bypasses....but we caught it in time and he got to live!

Recovery was tough for him. They wouldn't let my little bald self-stay with him at the hospital. We got him home eventually once all the tubes and wires came out and he felt well enough to walk on his own. Man, I feel like they rush you out awfully fast after such a major thing. Thank fully he is doing well to this day.

Chapter 46: One cancer obviously was not enough. Let's try another one

Ok, I know I get sassy about this, but I was barely out of the routine recovery phase when another cancer came knocking on my door. I mean for chrissake, I was just finishing up with the other cancer in 2021, and now I got diagnosed with another one in 2023. That was a little brisk pace, even for my buddies.

This time, it was primary CNS lymphoma. That's right, guys. This time, I had actual brain cancer. My brain was rapidly filled with so many tumors and swelling that I literally forgot who I was and collapsed into a coma at the time of my brain surgery. Talk about thankfully being in the right place at the right time! It was terrifying. I literally went from walking around Barnes and Noble killing time waiting to go check in for my brain surgery to not even knowing who I was, where I was, or what my birthday was as I was checking in for my brain surgery. It's like conscious me ceased to exist even though I was still standing upright.

Thank goodness the neurosurgeon happened to be walking through and gently convinced my frantic husband not to rush me to the or but to stay upstairs and have the surgery.

I actually did well after the surgery. Woke up smiling and everything...and then said hello to my husband, then rolled over and went encephalopathic and into a coma for a couple of days.

My poor brain was pissed off and full of swelling and seizing in defiance. Fortunately, my neuro team had the forethought to slam me with steroids and seizure meds, and when the seizing stopped and the swelling shrunk, I got to wake up days later.

I think of my poor husband, standing steadfast at my bedside, not leaving me for days, not giving up, and having to watch me literally disappear right in front of him. I am told that he kept yelling out to the nurses that they just had to save me, that this was the most beautiful, wonderful brain that they would ever meet and that it was worthy of being saved.

I think the world of that man. He is my hero, my best friend, and my favorite person in the whole world. I don't know what I would do without him. We are partners and we would do anything for each other, and that's how it should be.

This was one of the hardest battles I ever had to wage. Then I went the extra mile and did a stem cell transplant on top of all the chemo I already had to get rid of the cancer.

I was willing to do anything I had to do to try and keep cancer out of my life longer than just two years.

There was so much lonely time in the hospital. I was in there for a month at a time. My immune system was drained down to nothing. Despite getting multiple antibiotics, I got three different infections. It almost killed me to do it but I am telling myself that it is worth it. Anything that gives me the potential of having more time with my family is worth it in my book.

Chapter 47: I helped save my husband's life again

So, here we go again. I am in the middle of my second cancer battle and my poor husband has a terrible gallbladder attack.

He was actually in so much pain that he woke me up in the middle of the night. I was not technically allowed to even drive yet, but you bet your ass I flung him into the car and got him to the ER.

Yep, it was in fact his gallbladder, and everyone was scared to operate on him because he was on blood thinners. His surgeon understood the urgency of course but anesthesia was nervous.

I remained steadfast and said with a smile that we were not leaving until his gallbladder came out. I knew it was near to rupture and logically, I convinced them that it was better for the heart patient, with uncontrolled pain, to be operated on before it ruptured and he became septic.

So, with the helpful aid of clotting factors, platelets and ffp, he had his surgery and did well. And yes, his gallbladder was swollen and about to rupture.

Chapter 48: The day I finally told her off

As I was laying in the hospital for my second cancer and still fighting off stalking attempts from my mother, I finally decided it was time to tell her what I really thought and how much I wanted her to finally leave me alone for good.

Instead of sending a letter, I decided to send a text to her from my hospital bed. I am not sure why I picked this time to say things that were 30-plus years overdue to be said, but I decided to go for it.

I have decided not to share it word for word, but I will summarize it. I was eloquent, to the point, not cruel. I said things that were over 45 years overdue to be said.

In true mom style, she took that text, created what looked like something I sent in the mail, and sent copies to all her friends.

Am I upset or surprised by this? Unfortunately, no. And it did not stop her from trying to reach out to me or scam her way into my online sites. I just look at that as one more check in the box next to not reconsider letting her back into my life.

Do you know the only two words I never heard from my mother in my whole life are? I'm sorry. Never. Not once. Not one, darn, time. You know, I am such a softie that just hearing those two words...after everything....might have even made me reconsider kicking her out of my life. The one indicator that she has or had the slightest bit of remorse for anything would have actually meant the world to me.

Well, never mind. It never happened. I never heard the words. The end. It was somehow cathartic for me. It was in print. I know she received it. I will leave it at that.

Chapter 49: So why do I think of myself as a multitasker?

So, now I have become the ultimate multitasker. I am always doing multiple things at once.

I manage a full obgyn and aesthetics practice by myself. I am my own co-office manager.

I literally can't help myself but treat every moment as if it might be my last. I savor it. I am doing a million things at once. I am working in therapy on this because I need to get over that fear that I may not have more than one chance at everything.

Now, I am very active. I workout 4 times a week and bike 8 plus miles a day since my hemoglobin is not 7 anymore. I interact with people on a daily basis now that my immune system is regenerating.

I have a blog that talks about all the sensitive subjects that I update frequently.

I have multiple Facebook sites that I maintain and update regularly.

I have an Instagram that I update regularly.

I have a podcast on iHeart radio that I update regularly

I have an office website that includes everything about my business and practice, with plenty of personal patient testimonials that I use to help women every day.

Yep, I am pretty busy. Some might even say too busy but when you spent the better part of the last six months in the hospital, you feel like you have time to make up for it.

Chapter 50: What now?

What now? I'll tell ya what now. It's time to live. It's time to live without fear. It's time to not always be looking over your shoulder. It's time to not always freak out at the slightest pain or twinge. It is time to rejoice. It's time to travel. It's time to spread positivity as far as you can. It's time to use my experiences to help others. It's time to use these experiences with difficulty, pain, and evil and, turn them around, and use them as a light to guide others.

I have been to hell and back and back again. I have gotten through. I will not let it ruin me. I will not let it change who I am, or if it does, only change me for the stronger, wiser, and better.

No matter what has happened, I will never stop being thankful for who I am and where I am. Live every day to the fullest, folks. I know I will.

If you would like to know more about me or learn anything about the subjects people don't normally discuss, you can look me up in a number of ways.

Scan to Explore Social Links:

My other published works

OK, It's My Turn Now- a story of my first cancer battle

You Can't Make This Stuff Up- a funny narrative of my journey as an Obgyn for 25 years

You, Again? - the story of my second cancer battle

All of these can be found on amazon.com and a variety of other vendor sites.

www.ingramcontent.com/pod-product-compliance
Lightning Source LLC
Chambersburg PA
CBHW040747150426
42811CB00059B/1502